PLANT WITH GOD

90 DAILY DEVOTIONS FOR GROWING WITH JESUS

CASSANDRA LAWS

PLANTING WITH GOD

This book belongs ✝o:

PLANTING WITH GOD

Dedicated to
Jesus.

✝

For his children and my
sweet family.
Thank you lord for your
grace and mercy upon us.

Glory be to
God.

Ephesians 3:20-21

PLANTING WITH GOD

> "You are planting a garden, and that takes time to bloom."
> –God

Let us sit and relax in this garden of life with God surrounding our entire being.

Because through Jesus, that is where we can experience true peace, and it is such a gift. The best one we will ever get.
Thank you Jesus.

PLANTING WITH GOD

Introduction:

I joyfully invite you to come and sit with Jesus day by day as you let your worries fade and allow your faith to bloom.

Through God we can conquer the daily battles we were never meant to carry alone.

Your battles have already been won by Jesus on the cross, we just need to remind ourselves of this, directing our focus towards our Lord and Savior Jesus Christ daily.

Matthew 6:9-13

PLANTING WITH GOD

This devotional includes 90 days of devotions, along with prayers, bible verses, and inspiration all which God led me to while investing much time with him.

I pray this book may uplift your spirit. That with these words you find here you may also develop much trust, increase your faith, and allow solitude with God for growth in your daily walk.

"The sun shall shine bright on you, and in you as the Lord covers you with his love."
-Cassandra
@thewritersheis

May this bless you and many
others along the way.
All who believe and seek
God and his word daily shall flourish
and grow. Amen.

Psalm 92:12-15

PLANTING WITH GOD

Come to the garden
where we allow God to shower us with
his great love and protection.
Which is such a gift.

Prepare to grow with me, child.
–GOD

ISAIAH 58:11

THIS BOOK WAS CREATED FOR GOD'S CHILDREN TO
FIND PEACE THROUGH JESUS.
WHILE SITTING STILL IN HIS PRESENCE, YET GROWING
INTO SOMETHING INDESCRIBABLE AND BEYOND US.

GOD IS WHERE THE SUPPORT IS FOUND. LET IT BE JUST
YOU AND HIM TAKING A SEAT EVERY MORNING.
BE STILL. AS A PERSON WHO HAS OVERCOME ILLNESS
THROUGH GOD'S HEALING HAND,
NUMEROUS TRIALS AND YEARS OF BEING A CARETAKER,
GOD HAS PROVIDED ME THE ABILITY. HE HAS NEVER
LEFT ME.

THE EXPERIENCE IS PROFOUND AND WILL ALWAYS LEAD
YOUR DAY IN THE RIGHT WAY.

NO ONE PREPARES US FOR THE CHALLENGES THAT
COME WITH LIFE, BUT DON'T LET THAT DISCOURAGE
YOU, WE HAVE THE MOST AMAZING GUIDE THROUGH
GOD'S LOVE WHEN WE SEEK HIM.

Luke 10:21

PLANTING WITH GOD

KEEP CLIMBING YOUR WAY EVERYDAY WITH YOUR FACE LOOKING UPWARD TOWARDS JESUS. HE WILL HELP YOU THROUGH ANY CIRCUMSTANCE.

JESUS IS THE ONLY ONE THAT CAN MOVE OUR FEET, ACTIONS, THINKING AND DIRECTION WHEN WE CAN NO LONGER WALK, INSTEAD OF US BEING LED ASTRAY BY FLESHLY WAYS.

COLOSSIANS 2:6
As you have therefore received Christ Jesus the Lord, so walk in him.

PLANTING WITH GOD

Isaiah 40: 5-6 (nKJv)

The glory of the LORD shall be revealed, And all flesh shall see it together;

For the mouth of the Lord has spoken."

The voice said, "Cry out!" and he said, What shall I cry?"

"All flesh is grass, And all its loveliness is like the flower of the field."

PLANTING WITH GOD
DAY 1

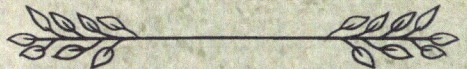

"You are planting a garden, and that takes time to bloom."

Isaiah 58:11 (nkjv)
The Lord will guide you continually and satisfy your soul in drought; and strengthen your bones; you shall be like a watered garden. And like a spring of water, whose waters do not fail.

I chose you specifically child, and I want to see you flourish in all the ways I created you to be. Now come and follow me, I will keep you shining bright and others will know it is me within you, always.

Deuteronomy 5:33

PLANTING WITH GOD
DAY 2

Dear child, sit still here with me. I know the days and nights are long, and you may feel alone and as if there is no one to call.

But wait, I am here. Allow your faith and belief to keep you close and with me as I, your father will guide you through each and every difficulty.

Therefore everyday call on me, and remember to always keep me near for I am the one who brings true healing and help, the world will never compare.

Psalm 46:10

Colossians 3:2

PLANTING WITH GOD
DAY 3

Let's talk, as you rest and tell me all your thoughts.

Share your worries here, you are safe with me.

I shall guide and protect every single thing of your being and experiences if you let me.

Stay a while, I just ask that you never become tired or weary with me.

As I carry the greatest plan, but my children must rest easy through me to understand.

PSALM 46:10
Hebrews 6:11

PLANTING WITH GOD
DAY 4

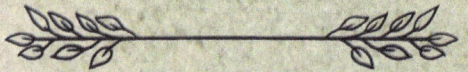

"In the waiting stay joyful. Pray. Give thanks and believe in the power of Jesus."
Colossians 1:11 (NIV)
Being strengthened with all power according to his glorious might so that you may have great endurance and patience

Trust in me and all I have in store for you.

This season shall not last forever, and soon you will know the reason for the waiting, and exactly why I chose you. Although I know it hasn't been easy for you. Keep coming back to me, and it will all make sense soon.

PLANTING WITH GOD
DAY 5

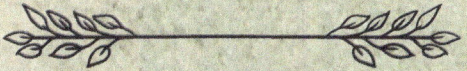

By my light, you shall find the path and the way with me. I can't promise this narrow road will be easy. As life on earth wasn't made to be easy but rather lived navigating it closely with me. Choosing me over everything.

Not everyone can withstand this walk, as they do not call out to me and wait. I've seen and watched. I call out to them only to find them wondering the other way lost.

The growth you'll find with me will be beyond your greatest dreams. Although it may not be easy, I promise, I will never let you wonder lost if you cling to me.

PSALM 56:3;
MATTHEW 6:34;
JAMES 1:3

PLANTING WITH GOD
DAY 6

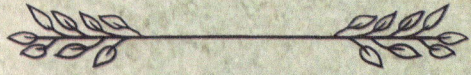

When I must get your attention, I hope you understand, as my children keep running away from me. "Hear", I am calling them to sit, rest and stay close to me. "Cling to me in all you do." If everything was easy, what would be your need for me? And what comforts would this world ever bring you.

JAMES 1:2 (nkjv)
My brethren, count it all joy when you fall into various trials.

Psalm 63:1

PLANTING WITH GOD
DAY 7

May you find my lamp everywhere you go, so you don't get lost in this darkened place. The light can seem dim if you don't hold on to me.

Remember, if you can't find your lamp easily, keep seeking me deeply, and I'll guide you to it. With this world light is difficult to find as the world has become so darkened by all those who turn away from me. Allow the stillness and quietness through me to keep you all the days, that is my presence within you. BE the peace, love and the light this world needs.

Psalm 29:11
Colossians 3:14
Psalm 26:11

PLANTING WITH GOD
DAY 8

Colossians 2:5 (nkjv)
For though I am absent in the flesh, yet I am with you in spirit, rejoicing to see your good order and the steadfastness of your faith in Christ.

Lord, we will trust, believe and wait on you. For your plans will always overcome ours.
The direction you lead us in may not make sense but I will trust it.

I will recall your name always and rejoice in the goodness and gladness of you Jesus.
Amen, thank you Father God.

Jeremiah 29:11

PLANTING WITH GOD
DAY 9

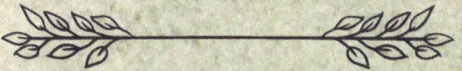

Some search a lifetime yet think they can't find me. They go this way or that way, but none ever stop to ask me the direction they should take. They keep moving along searching, as if I am visible to see. Then reaching out to worldly things, these will never satisfy my children. However, the attempts are continuous, and here I am waiting for them to trust me.

Yet they still cannot find me as they keep running, lost. But those who stop running and turn to seek to know me, shall find me through the stillness, waiting and reading my word daily, and they shall know and hear me all of their days.

Jeremiah 42:3; Psalm 18:1
John 15:5; Proverbs 22:12

PLANTING WITH GOD
DAY 10

Each day is a day of its own.
Upon awakening guard yourself with me and do not fret about the days before or behind you. For when you place your focus on me, the here and the now, you can prepare yourself for gardening. Though you must water and feed yourself daily with me or you will lose yourself in this world and in the daily tasks that most place before me.

Allow me to do my work and lead your day. Some get distracted that they forget all about me. I love my children so very much. But they have usually gone on about their day without me. Therefore missing out on many great opportunities. And here I stay waiting for them to call out to me. Invite me in, I will never interrupt, but I certainly will show you the way.

Matthew 7:7-8
Psalm 107:29
Matthew 6:34

PLANTING WITH GOD
DAY 11

"Give me your burdens, hand it all over to me.
And you, child, shall walk in peace."

Psalm 18:1 (nkjv)
I will love you, o Lord, my strength.

2 Samuel 22:29 (nkjv)
"For you are my lamp, o Lord, the Lord shall enlighten my darkness.
Amen.
Thank you Jesus.

Lord, you truly allow my petals to keep, and not wither. My life to bloom all from a seed that grew in my heart to be watered by you.
So that I may live and grow only by following you.

PLANTING WITH GOD
DAY 12

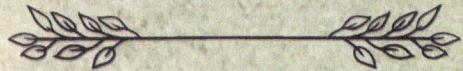

Rise, and rise again. Rejoice in the Lord. Give Jesus all the praise and the Glory. Regardless of the circumstances, know that I am near and all you have to do is keep close and call out to me daily.

"There isn't a day I made that you wouldn't need me."

Matthew 11:28 (nKJv)
Come to me, all you
who labor and are heavy laden,
and I will give you
rest.

"God will
provide
the "rest".
EXODUS 33:14

PLANTING WITH GOD
DAY 13

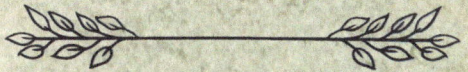

Talk with me, you can tell me anything. I already know your thoughts, your ways and most especially your heart. Your desires, and fears. Trust that I only want what is best for my children.

As your heavenly father I understand your troubles, child. I know in this world it is hard for my children to come and sit or even find rest.
For you to do so now means so much to me. Watch how your day flows freely when you sit still and rest in me. I will never disappoint.

Luke 12:25-26

PLANTING WITH GOD
DAY 14

If you need to cry, weep in my arms. My arms are always open for you.

Wait here a while if you need to. Some of my children will experience much at a time. Which is calling them to find the rest they so badly need, yet they keep going to find themselves on empty struggling to do even the smallest task.

Come, rest your soul with me and you shall be renewed, able to conquer all that you need to do with me.

Psalm 55:16;
Jeremiah 31:25

PLANTING WITH GOD
DAY 15

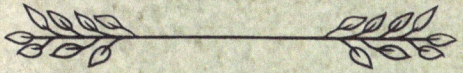

I have watched and seen while you have stood upright when the breeze rushed in. The storm hit with a vengeance. Yet your faith never stumbled, and your soul never perished as you walked right through it with me.

You grew in it, knowing with me you can conquer anything. Armored and prepared for such a time, and any time like this when you choose me.

Psalm 107:29 (nkjv)
He calms the storm,
so that its waves are
still.

PLANTING WITH GOD
DAY 16

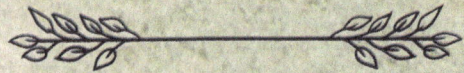

The waiting room is where you will find me. You have to be willing, otherwise you will think I am no where to be found.

There isn't much else for you to do except to call out to me, and I will always be here for you. I never leave. However, its my children who run from me, chasing worldly things then losing it all; when simply they need me and will have all they've been seeking.

I recall the days when you used the waiting room to worry, now you pick up the bible and pray to me. Life is much easier this way, you see?

The peace you find while you wait allows so much grace to take place.

John 14:27

PLANTING WITH GOD
DAY 17

Don't waste the waiting in your secret place, let it be where you come to find me to escape the worldly things. As the place you wait decides your steps and in my arms waiting is the place you will wish to stay. There will be no delays when you wait this way.

I know you feel alone some days and as if I have taken too long. Please know that with many great opportunities, can also come great harm. Your father will never rush you into something that is not good too soon. Only the best I send to my children and some times that requires you to bloom while conquering heavy storms with me before you do. I teach much patience in the secret place for the best has yet to come on your journey with me.

Romans 8:25

PLANTING WITH GOD
DAY 18

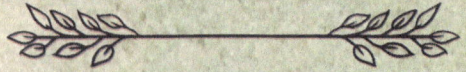

Every second and moment of waiting with me will be worth it, you will see. Oh Child, please hear me.

While we wait, let's pray, in any way you need to pray. In whatever way that works best for you. You can speak it quietly or internally, write to me or just cry with me. Whatever you need, I will be there
with you.
For by quieting your mind,
you can hear me
more clearly to truly know
truly I am with you.

Colossians 4:2;
Psalm 119:50

PLANTING WITH GOD
DAY 19

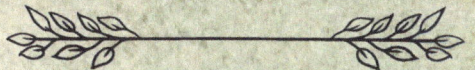

I speak loudly yet to deafened ears it seems; I am saddened by those who don't know me. I have created and conquered the world, I can conquer anything, but the belief and faith is lost to the flesh. They don't wait with me. Do they not trust me? My children want it all, but are they truly ready, will you keep me close when you do have it all? I check the heart so make sure your wants are pure and your promises are kept, to receive it you must believe. I already go before you, but you must not leave, take every step with me.

Come, let us pace throughout your garden to build a plan you will keep. As we discuss all I have in store for you and the steps that you need to get to where I have called you to be. Child, your plans I know, and I have so much for you so follow very closely.

Matthew 28:20;
Romans 8:6

PLANTING WITH GOD
DAY 20

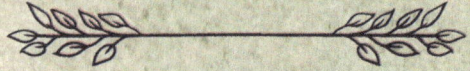

Reach out grab my hand for I have prepared the plan.
But which path will you choose? My hand reaches out to you so freely. I ask that you take a hold of it to experience what true love and peace is.
Now let us take a walk together in your garden to see what work we need to do today. Tell me all that is bothering you or any obstacles that may be in your way. My plan can be easily interrupted by this world, yet, most don't trust in all I can do to make it work out for your good.

You'll find there is always great work to do with me to prosper you in your walk. The more you come to me, I can help things flourish beautifully.

Psalm 92:13; Psalm 138:3; John 13:13

PLANTING WITH GOD
DAY 21

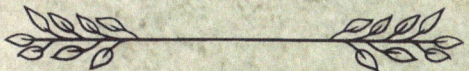

Let's talk for a while, dear child. If you seek me, you will end up finding everything you need. You'll discover answers easily. You will find your way and be covered by my armor which is all you will need for any battle along the way.

I have absolutely everything you need. The energy you invest in worrying, place that energy into me, seeking me, and my truth. You will gladly find me internally. Everywhere you go, you'll be filled with the holy spirit and know that I am there helping you along the way.

Psalm 119:133;
1 Chronicles 16:27

PLANTING WITH GOD
DAY 22

I see you every morning, wondering if this will be the day for you. Will this finally be it. A miracle or a dream come true.

Questioning if you will figure out the way, but don't forget to stop and remember me. I am the way. You may pray, question, and cry over it, yet simply take a moment to sit with me through it.

Please remember you are my child, questions, cries, problems—bring them to me.

As I provide solutions, joy and peace through any circumstance.

You are not alone, I am with you. Carry me closely, otherwise the faith you need will not be able to exist if you travel without me.

1 Peter 1:5-6; 1 Peter 1:2; Psalm 31:5

PLANTING WITH GOD
DAY 23

My light leads, as with the Holy Spirit, there is always a lamp carrying you along the way.

Most don't believe unless they can "see", in which they cannot at least yet anyway. However, if they come to me, and keep seeking they will see me in other ways.

If you were to recall your darkest days, there was still a glimpse of light you kept seeking to find.

You had to return back to me to acknowledge you still carry that light, however, it only shines bright with me.
It had been dimmed by this world.
And you may not always see that light, but you are shining it for someone else and unknowingly growing from it; as you navigate life and garden with me while planting seeds.

Matthew 5:15-16
Psalm 18:28

PLANTING WITH GOD
DAY 24

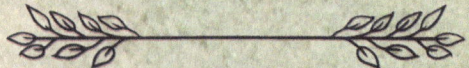

Trust me, you'll want to be on this journey with me. I am not saying your path will be perfect or easy. There will be difficulties, but if you let me I will lead you perfectly. I will show you in which way you should walk and even what to say. Who you need to reach, and exactly what you should do with anything you face.

Do you trust me? I know my children go out thinking no one cares or maybe even think I am not coming to help. This journey takes much faith. You must believe for it all to take place, that's when belief becomes enough because you know you would have never accomplished or won this battle without me. That's when my children know waiting patiently to watch me work is worth all the waiting it can take. So please stay with me each and every day.

Hebrews 6:12

PLANTING WITH GOD
DAY 25

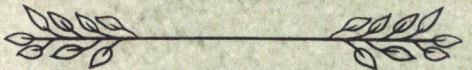

I have found my children love the easy route, they choose the other direction which doesn't include stopping to ask me or waiting. I teach as we wait together. The reason for this is so you can learn many things. This is important for all that is to come day to day. If you don't learn something through your waiting and experience, how will you be prepared for the next?

As any parent should say, I have asked and taught but some may just need to find their way. Their way back to the truth. I have spoken, yet they do not hear. Oh, but if they'd just stop and listen, they should know I am the way to safety. That's all any parent would want is their child to be led to the correct path and stay out of dangers way. To be healthy and protected, I want that badly for all my children. But the flesh and this world is consuming the way,

1 Peter 4:3
Matthew 6:21

PLANTING WITH GOD
DAY 26

Be cautious of your own way as the direction can lead you astray into dangers way. So come, let's have discussions every day, read my word in the bible as it is your road map for this life here on earth.

Ask for understanding, guidance, love and protection through me and you shall gain these things. Please understand this is a relationship we are building. And although I love you always, to keep you close we must work closely daily.

Do not let your flesh choose your way, as I love you dearly so here you must stay with me safe everyday.

Proverbs 14:16;
Proverbs 14:26

PLANTING WITH GOD
DAY 27

The circumstances and trials or all you may be experiencing today does not define you child.

I have defined you since the beginning, perfectly knit with every part of you designed by me.

Yet this world has ripped my precious children away and shattered so many. Despite this, remember you were mine to keep from the beginning.

I will restore and renew you, even if you must repent again and again until you find that in me is where life truly begins. To live joyful and glad through me no matter what life may bring. And just as you want to see your family and loved ones happy. I desire so much the same. Come let us walk in gratitude and thankfulness today.

1 Thessalonians 5:16-18.
Acts 3:19
Isaiah 59:1

PLANTING WITH GOD
DAY 28

Silence and peace within, everyone seeks. Not knowing it is found here with me, and the holy spirit within. When you are looking for what you need to make it through the firestorms that may come day to day. You can find me within, call out to me, and I will be the fire you need to carry you above the flames and keep you safe. By my flame you will walk right through it unharmed, untouched. That's the protection I provide. You will be amazed at the the path you take all by just sitting in my presence which simply comes from within by calling out to me.

Psalm 62:5:
My soul, waits silently for
God alone,
for my expectation
is from him.

PLANTING WITH GOD
DAY 29

Rain or sunshine I am here and always near. My child, don't only call on me when there is a storm. If there is such fear and no faith, how can I only exist then for I am not a God of fear, but of power and love which will always be needed from above. I am to be remembered daily as your work was never for this world, it's with me. Therefore if you don't speak with me daily as you would your boss or co-workers and friends, how can I lead your path clearly or even take part in your day when you don't invite me in. What kind of team would we make?

My children come to me when in need but forget to take the time to communicate with me daily, then wonder why they continue to be led astray.

Isaiah 41:13

PLANTING WITH GOD
DAY 30

When and if you feel alone, come to me.
Let us sit and pick through
your garden, so you don't wilt but grow
by faith alone. Let's see
what needs watering and pruning today
so that fear is not in the
way of all the growth that needs
to take place.
Remember I will never
leave you in this alone. I will
always be here sitting awaiting
your call at my throne.

Dear child,
I am always with you.
Love,
God

Deuteronomy 31:8

PLANTING WITH GOD
DAY 31

Seek to know me. Be still in the presence of me. Never forget to pray,
call out to me and believe while you await my rescue at any time and
on any day. Trust my timing as it is always specifically chosen for your sake.

The work you'll do comes easily when you simply sit with me.

You may think you're not accomplishing anything however remember you'll conquer much in the waiting.

Let the quiet and stillness with me be your way, and your guide and light to shine through each and every new day.

Proverbs 3:6
Micah 6:8

PLANTING WITH GOD
DAY 32

Dear child, I will always allow you to preserve the energy, time and effort you may later need by resting in me.

Spend time with me, just being still more frequently while learning to listen and wait for me does more than wasting energy by not being close to me. Going this way or that way will only make you feel lost.

"For it is only I who can help you. So cling to me." Never think I will forget thee. For you my children are so special and important to me.

And remember the answers come in the waiting.

"I teach through your listening. My gifts come more easily, to those who wait on me."

Isaiah 33:2
Psalm 35:9

PLANTING WITH GOD
DAY 33

Prayer to our Heavenly Father

Oh, dear Father God, you know all I am experiencing. Please help me to hear you. Guide me to where I am supposed to be and help me to live through you only. I pray for knowledge of your will for me and the power to carry it out.
I cry out to you for this and believe you will guide me always if I trust in you and have faith.
Thank you Jesus.
I pray you may allow the Holy Spirit to fill my presence and being so that I may continue to do your will always.
In Jesus' mighty name I pray, amen.
Thank you God.

Matthew 6:9-13

John 14:26

PLANTING WITH GOD
DAY 34

"You will triumph, for when you call out to me, evil must flee. You will no longer suffer in agony when you are with me."

Remember, I lead the way, there's no need to overthink about this day, the past or time to come. As this adds worries by not fully relying on me which will only cause you to use up the energy that should be preserved to follow me.

Trust in me fully, for humans will be set in their ways and fail. Yet I will forever be the same yesterday, today and tomorrow, my promises remain.

During this time you may feel overwhelmed but just know I overcame this world and can overcome anything.

Jeremiah 33:3
Hebrews 13:8
Isaiah 60:15

PLANTING WITH GOD
DAY 35

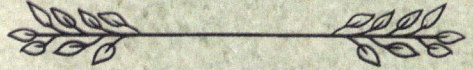

I see you child, all the suffering, the trials, the heartache, the pain. All of this was never meant for you to carry, especially when it all can bring such hurt and shame that doesn't allow my children to move forward.

Through it all use it as an opportunity to grow and learn to live through me.

If you believe and learn to fully trust me, I will lead you out of this dark place and to answers along the way. All your heart desires will be met in such a loving way. I promise misery cannot live in the place I have for you to stay.

Romans 8:18
Psalm 34:4
2 Thessalonians 3:5

PLANTING WITH GOD
DAY 36

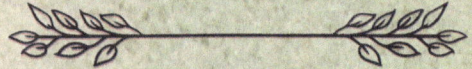

My children wonder lost thinking
I don't exist, yet if they'd choose me
instead of worldly things –they would then see
me. Seek to find me through everything, I will
be with you and you will know it is me.
You belong to me,
therefore any time you have a need for me
know my help is on the way, I am always one
call or cry away. Wait on me.
Bring all of you to me.
Release your worries, doubts and fears, lay it
all down. Take it out of your hands and pass it
over to me.
As I have already carried it
all but you keep pulling it back into
your hands, it's time to let go
and take my hand.

Psalm 16:11
Matthew 21:22

PLANTING WITH GOD
DAY 37

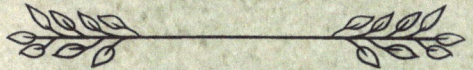

On earth comes free will and it isn't easy for the flesh. Coming to me is a great choice and the greatest decision you will ever make. When you take the direction to follow me—your life shall be a prize to many. Everything about you, and who you were once believed to be will change. All for my glory, to be all I intended you to be here on this journey with me.

This isn't the typical route for others to choose or take, and I am proud of you child.
Your eyes will begin to open, the darkness will fade and your being and purpose will now make sense to you along the way.

Choose me, as my way, my path
leads many out of misery.

John 14:29
Acts 3:26
Psalm 37:7

PLANTING WITH GOD
DAY 38

Walking along in this life with me, you'll find such meaning. Through storms you'll find showers that lead to new life and existence. After the showers fade the sunshine comes to brighten your day for you to grow mightily and move forward through me.

Although hard to understand now, but when it feels heavy, just wait, my light will guide you always. That sunshine after the rain is the light you carry from me within. And soon joy and happiness will cover you while you are with me. There will be no time for anything that brings you down as I can only rise you up, dear child.

I know it doesn't make sense today. But the day it does you won't be able to comprehend how much your outlook and life has changed. Because in the end you find your purpose through the pain. To overcome it all with God, for your Father's glory.
And there will be absolutely
no shame for the struggles you
faced.

Psalm 16:11
Isaiah 60:20

PLANTING WITH GOD
DAY 39

You will learn much
with me if you allow yourself to
stop fretting about matters of the world and
instead let me move in more freely.
Learning is a process of teachings, and
experience brings growth and much patience.
You child, have the greatest teacher with you
if you choose God today.
The process of learning doesn't always feel great.
Plant yourself with me
and watch all we can grow
here in this place where trouble
will no longer sprout.
Now protected while I surround
your spirit and soul always.

My beautiful child your flowers
shall spring up and bloom forever
with me.

Isaiah 35:2
2 Peter 3:18

PLANTING WITH GOD
DAY 40

There is so much to be known and learned while you are planted here with me, but how will my children experience it or ever know if they don't come and plant themselves with me.

Let the sprinkles of hope I bring, hold you close. I see what happens is my children are chosen from the very day I created you. Yet life led alone without me leads them astray directly into dangers way. They are robbed from their time and need for me, and it's not their fault because if they weren't taught how can they know any other way.

I have such a plan and purpose for you. The pain this life can bring creates a need for me and such a relationship for us to build together each day. It becomes such a beautiful thing that will absolutely be worth all the waiting. As your need for me will outweigh all the misery the world can bring, I promise you.

James 1:1-13
Romans 8:28
Psalms 139:13-15

PLANTING WITH GOD
DAY 41

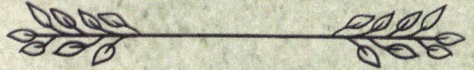

I will show you the truth about yourself and all you were created to be. I know right now it feels tough, as if you don't know what to do or who you are supposed to be. You may feel alone, but here you are, with an option and that is me. Exactly where I needed you to be secluded so that you can finally hear, find and KNOW me.

PSALM 46:10

Romans 8:28 (nKJv)
And we know that God causes everything to work together for the good of those who love God and are called according to his purpose for them.

PLANTING WITH GOD
DAY 42

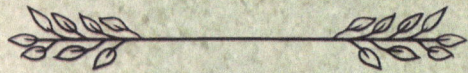

You were born with such a gift
of purpose that somehow was stolen from you
along the way.
The world can do so much
damage; this is why it is best to
stay close to me.
I'll show you the truth about you
and all I created you to be.

The Lord says:
"Keep me with you always."
Some search a lifetime for
their "safe place" and peace.
Not knowing this is only found through me.
Now may you allow me to plant you
in places that are beyond your
greatest dreams.
What all I had planned
for you initially."

Psalm 33:11
Ephesians 1:11
Proverbs 3:5-6

PLANTING WITH GOD
DAY 43

I can see you think
this journey with me is too big for you,
oh child that's why I chose you.
I already knew you'd be prepared
for this walk.

It was I that called and you listened and sought. Therefore here we are and the mission I set before you will not send you into despair like the times before when this world greatly failed you and sent you away from my care.
Yet you saw I had always been there and in that you trusted. And now your faith will bloom.
Watch it flourish you anywhere you are planted with me. Your flowers have bloomed all for my glory
because of you.

Ephesians 3:20-21

PLANTING WITH GOD
DAY 44

"One day you'll look back and know all you have experienced in this life was never a mistake. I will forever be your saving grace as I have been here from the beginning. You just had to find your way back to me."

Come to me as you are, not as who others want you to be. I love you so much, child."

-God

Joshua 1:9 (nkjv)

Have I not commanded you? Be strong and of good courage; do not be afraid, nor be dismayed, for the LORD your God is with you wherever you go."

PLANTING WITH GOD
DAY 45

If you wait to come to me in perfection, you will miss out on the opportunity to truly know me, and the promises I have in store for you. For it is God who shines light so you can grow. I water your roots deep like a plant in the sea. I will shower many blessings upon you if you choose me and walk in all I created you to be.

"Rather than worry, why not believe and invest your energy in being hopeful in me. Bringing me with you each day to make it a smooth walk for you and others you bring along the way.

I make it easy for my children to come to me. All you need to do is call and listen for the directions that I may quietly whisper back to you, deep in your spirit. I need your full attention on me."
Love, God

Matthew 6:34; Jeremiah 42:3

PLANTING WITH GOD
DAY 46

Child, why do you fear so much? With me you'll never walk alone again. Surrounded by me through the Holy Spirit and my angel army. Your internal peace will confirm this. Your flesh can be deceiving, so don't be fooled. Choose my way, then go out, be bold, and brave as with me you are safe.

"For with me, fear cannot live. Pick up your cross and follow me."
-God

Matthew 16:24-26 (nkjv)
Then Jesus said to His disciples, "If anyone desires to come after Me, let him deny himself, and take up his cross, and follow Me. 25 For whoever desires to save his life will lose it, but whoever loses his life for My sake will find it. 26 For what profit is it to a man if he gains the whole world, and loses his own soul? Or what will a man give in exchange for his soul?

PLANTING WITH GOD
DAY 47

Here we are today, I hope you've noticed the change in you. As I see it too. May the seeds we've planted come as a reminder that you're growing with me each new day.

We have planted my word, love, mustard seeds of faith, trust, hope and buried pain.
All to find it takes much time to bloom into something that is beyond you.

Keep planting and you will look around one day at such a beautiful peaceful place you would have never believed could be.
And that is found through me.

I am so proud of you for walking my way, and for seeking me everyday. This journey and all the pruning isn't easy, yet it is the best thing my children could ever learn to do.

PSALM 25:10 (nKJv)
All the paths of the lord
are mercy and truth.
To such as keep his
covenant and his
testimonies.

PLANTING WITH GOD
DAY 48

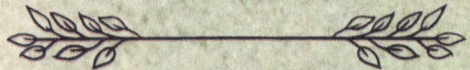

For I know all that is troubling you and I will take it off of your hands. All you have to do is hand it over and walk with me, listen for me, let me guide you to places that are unseen.

With me you shall not know the answers too soon, it's a lesson from me to you. You see the steps I take you on are a journey to save you, never to harm you. If my child does not learn, he must keep growing further and further in my word.

Some miss this opportunity, believe in me and you will learn soon. Please don't ever allow me to lose you.

My child you are very dear to me.

2 Corinthians 1:3-4

PLANTING WITH GOD
DAY 49

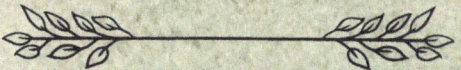

Remind your loved ones, brothers and sisters and everyone you have the opportunity to meet of my love. Encourage them to also take a moment each day to sit and invite me in. That is the purpose of why these words have been written. Especially those experiencing trials and pain. For them to truly experience me, they must seek to know me, and I will reveal my truth.

I am here to stay but some flee and run away from their father God. The flesh is weak but the Holy Spirit is strong. Keep walking with me no matter how hard it is and just you watch each and every word and great promise come to pass in your life.

This is the way to planting yourself with God, where I allow your seeds to grow into such purpose and beauty.

1 John 4:7–12

PLANTING WITH GOD
DAY 50

My hope is finally, all
of my children surrender to me.
To run towards Christ Jesus. Surrendering pain, worries, and the antagonizing feelings that keep my children away. Lost, getting no where, seeking help from a world that would never have God's capabilities to truly help, hear, listen and change things in a moment.

Here I am. My great love and help freely available,
I have already carried it for you all.
Yes you. Jesus will always carry you.

So come, lay it all down for me and yourself child. You deserve what I have intended for your life and this load was never meant to be carried only by you.

1 Peter 5:6-10
James 4:7
Romans 12:1

PLANTING WITH GOD
DAY 51

Song of Solomon 2:12

And here we are you see, in seeking and finding me you are growing.
A new seed I planted for you, with roots tough and sturdy to bloom. Now to become I called you to be. Don't miss these daily opportunities with me.

PLANTING WITH GOD
DAY 52
Philippians 4:7

May you find that moments with me are pure bliss. Don't let our time be missed. Worrying will keep you stuck in that place which doesn't allow for you to flourish and fully bloom. My children can have many moments with me, however, some will not hear because they do not seek to grow with me. But if you do, you will find such peace. Faith is all you need for it all to come true.

PLANTING WITH GOD
DAY 53
Ephesians 3:19

Rest easy here with me. May you find yourself wrapped in my arms. All the love and protection you could ever need is found through me. Don't seek love from a world that doesn't recognize truth and their creator. Through me is where all the love and happiness lives always. Others may show love but they will never love you like Jesus does.

PLANTING WITH GOD
DAY 54
Matthew 11:28-30

As you bloom don't forget to remember me daily. Life will happen but worry not, it is not over yet. All has been overcome at the cross. Open my word and seek the answers you need there with me. Throughout anything you go through, I promise to be with you. Pray, believe, relax and read, that's all I ask of you.

PLANTING WITH GOD
DAY 55
Jeremiah 29:13-14

Seek me and all that was a mystery you will see. By spending time with me daily more and more will be revealed. You'll be surprised at such growth opportunities some miss not knowing me.

PLANTING WITH GOD
DAY 56

John 1:4 nkjv
**In him was life, and the
life was the light of men.**
Child look at that sunshine coming in.
Shining over and within, with this
light darkness cannot exist. Oh the growth
I see in you. Truly beautifully revealed and placed by
me. The things you will do in this life with me
planted deep within.

PLANTING WITH GOD
DAY 57

Shower and feed your soul with my word each day. Some come plant their seeds they wait a little, then flee or wither away. Doubting, with such little faith forgetting to care for themselves they fade into weeds unsettled allowing themselves to be picked apart by this world. If they'd care for their growth, as a good gardener would, their plants and soil would bloom into much.

Jeremiah 15:16

PLANTING WITH GOD
DAY 58

On days when it feels like too much to take, lay it all down for me. I will come help you garden. Showering you with my love as you sit and listen. Your growth comes from me, and deep within, grounding and planting your heart exactly where it needs to be. I chose you particularly for a purpose that you will find by traveling with me.

John 14:13-14

PLANTING WITH GOD
DAY 59

Life is hard child, I know.
You've experienced sunshine, rain, clouds and pain, especially throughout your journey much life has been traveled. I know as I have traveled along with you. Many of my children don't just appear in this way willing and ready to follow me fully. I am proud of you for stopping to come and grow through me as now it's time to rest while I restore every bit of what was lost in the storm and heavy rainfall.

1 Peter 5:10

PLANTING WITH GOD
DAY 60

You see the others planted beside you so quiet and growing. Some fast, some slow—they sit and meditate with me. They will also surround and support you as I do. This journey may seem quiet and lonely, not often the route many take here planted with me. You may start to notice some fade and some stay. Those that stay with me shall live and have everlasting life and joy. Please know I don't expect perfection, just a relationship and partnership each day.

Psalm 73:28

PLANTING WITH GOD
DAY 61

To remain close to me is the absolute best thing you could do, not only for you but those around you, family and generations to come. If they all find and have me, they have all the help they could ever need. Not only that but protection as well. With all that goes on today in this world, it's best to keep me close always.

1 Chronicles 22:19

PLANTING WITH GOD
DAY 62

Growth and healing truly takes love, time and much work with me. It is worth it, you'll see. Did you know that during it you can find great rest through me? Rest in me and I can assure you, the outcome is beyond anything you could have dreamed. The peace in it allows much healing to my children and you are strengthened by all of it.

Psalm 91:9-14

PLANTING WITH GOD
DAY 63

Will you always need to be showered by me. Let me ask you, what would this earth be like if I never watered it? You would think dry, cracked, suffering and dying. Screaming for nurturing. This is how impactful and important it is to be watered and fed by me daily.

John 4:14

Psalm 63:1

PLANTING WITH GOD
DAY 64

Remember, when all else is failing, handing it over to God will never fail you. Each time you have fallen, you may not realize it but if you are breathing today I have always lifted you up from those falls.
Every time.
Why? PURPOSE. You have much purpose through me, child.

Psalm 37:23-24

PLANTING WITH GOD
DAY 65

Your worth in me shall not wilt nor fade. When you are with me and trouble arises, remember it has already been overcome. Jesus gave it all for you. Every obstacle can be conquered through and by Jesus. I will take over the trouble, and you will succeed the test by trusting me.

John 16:33

PLANTING WITH GOD
DAY 66

When days come that make
your walk difficult with me because
life happens over and over
it seems. Come to me always.
Remember that anger, hurt and resentment
could never fix anything, but fully watering and
feeding your soul with me each day will resolve
everything. It is the nourishment my children
need.

Psalm 46:1

PLANTING WITH GOD
DAY 67

Let me ask child, when you see something beautiful, do you ever wonder what all it took to create it?

A life even, as Jesus gave his own life for you. The work of my hands will never create anything that isn't pure and beautifully made, which is exactly the way I see you. I look upon you and smile, as I watch the beauty and work of my hands bloom through you and all who surround you.

Ecclesiastes 3:11

PLANTING WITH GOD
DAY 68

What many miss is they come in and earnestly yearn to know me. In their hearts the seed is planted but they keep holding onto it seeking somewhere to plant it in this world. Yet it doesn't fit or grow anywhere. They don't understand that seed deeply rooted within belongs to me in my hand. To be planted sturdy in my soil and showered by me. Otherwise what growth can become of a fallow seed.

1 Corinthians 3:6-9

PLANTING WITH GOD
DAY 69

You worry much about your
family and the ones you love, I see.
Your heart is pure in its way, and desires
the best for all who may stay when you
have gone away. But did you know the
greatest gift you can leave today is the gift of seeking
to fully know me. Sharing and leaving this great gift is
more than money could ever provide. This amount of
richness can never be spent fully nor will it be taken
away.

                              Proverbs 13:22
                              Ephesians 1:4-14

PLANTING WITH GOD
DAY 70

As you have walked page by page here with me here, I hope my dear child that you have an understanding of my love and your need for me. Learning how to further yourself in this walk with me. It simply takes a tiny mustard seed of faith to be planted in my soil. Your belief will fuel your soul, and your flowers will grow. You will begin to blossom and bloom as the seasons change. My love for you will never fade.

Philippians 1:6

PLANTING WITH GOD
DAY 71

From the Author:

It has been such a joy to create this book with Jesus, and to be on this journey with you. My brothers and sisters in Christ, I pray you find much meaning, trust, hope, faith and growth throughout these pages. Oh the love of Jesus poured out to me through these words, all from sitting still with him. I encourage you to quiet your mind and seek God fully today.

PSALM 16:11

PLANTING WITH GOD
DAY 72

From the Author:

When I first arrived in the secret place finally truly seeking God, I was beat down by life and our circumstances. Tired, upset and worried as sickness overcame myself and my family due to several incurable illnesses, and other life challenges. However, although things haven't been perfect God is faithful with his word. Please note, we don't always come in perfect and he doesn't expect that. He will meet you right where you are and offer his hand of healing, all we have to do is take a hold of it. My time with God, has provided us the hope, strength and healing we needed to survive this life we were given. Jesus will carry us all through.

Psalm 118:17

Galatians 2:20

PLANTING WITH GOD
DAY 73

Isaiah 41:10 (NIV)

"So do not fear, for I am with you; do not be dismayed, for I am your God. I will strengthen you and help you; I will uphold you with my righteous right hand"

PLANTING WITH GOD
DAY 74

Don't miss the moments and growth through Jesus that can be so easily found in the waiting. The secret place is where we can plant ourselves. To grow in the promise of all he has in store for us, and who he called us to be and do for his Glory. It is truly incredible, by being obedient and remaining still, building a relationship with him; our lives can be rearranged. Our strength and bodies renewed and our spirit fulfilled. Now to glorify and pray to our father God in the next few pages.

-Cassandra
(@thewritersheis)

PLANTING WITH GOD
DAY 75

Prayer for Guidance

Dear father God,
Lord thank you for another day
lord, thank you for your grace, love and
mercy on me.
Lord, I pray you may lead my
way today, in all that I do,
help me to follow you.
I pray my questions, concerns
and worries may reach you first
before I travel on my own.
Lord guide my thinking, actions,
mind, direction and steps so that I may
stay on this path with you.
Help me to know where to go and
all I need to do to serve you and
the Kingdom today.
In Jesus' mighty name
I pray Amen.
Thank you lord Jesus.

Psalms 25:4-5

PLANTING WITH GOD
DAY 76

Prayer for Repentance

Dear Father God, thank you for loving me as I am. Lord, I pray and cry out for your forgiveness for any sins I have made, and due to my fleshly ways. I will continue to repent throughout my days. Remembering that you have washed these away, yet I should yield to sin.

Lord, I ask you for forgiveness. I pray you mold me into who you need me to be to prepare me for your Kingdom come each and every day. And through you, I pray for a heart of love and forgiveness of others also. Thank you for such love and mercy that is beyond me.
You are worthy of all honor and praise always.
In Jesus' mighty name I pray.
Amen.
Thank you God.

Acts 3:19; Psalm 25:6-7; Matthew 6:9-13

PLANTING WITH GOD
DAY 77
Prayer for Forgiveness

Dear Father God,
Lord I pray you may help me
have a heart of forgiveness toward
others. If there is anything you
have taught us, it is the love you have for your
children regardless.
Lord, in this world I have many regrets that
I know you Jesus have overcome for me.
Father, I cannot thank you enough. Therefore,
I should not expect others to act out of
perfection, I pray for those who have acted
out of flesh towards me. I pray to carry a
forgiving heart full of love towards all. This
world may have hurtful people, yet I don't
have to hurt them further nor do I have to
carry a hurting heart as I know that is not
what you have provided in me. God, help me
forgive and love fully.
In Jesus' mighty name, I pray,
Amen.
Thank you Jesus.

Luke 23:34-38

PLANTING WITH GOD
DAY 78

Prayer for Illness, Trials & Pain

Dear Father God,
oh Lord, I know you hear and see my heart and hurting. Lord, I am in suffering everyday. Father heal us as we navigate these circumstances.
Lord, hear our cries in our suffering and relieve us of this pain dear Lord. We pray for complete healing, and assistance from you to allow for relief, peace and love as we go through this time with you by our side.
Lord, this suffering is hindering my walk, please lord make it flee in the mighty name of Jesus. I pray I will heal and be strengthened in my weakness by Christ Jesus.
Lord minister to me while I sit with you during this difficult time. Amen.
Thank you God.

**Isaiah 40:29; Psalm 30:2;
2 Timothy 2:3**

PLANTING WITH GOD
DAY 79

Prayer for Distress

Dear Father God, I come to you in my distress Lord. I hand over my worries to you and pray you may answer me on how to resolve what I am going through. I pray I may find peace and growth throughout this process with you.

Lord, I find it hard to focus as my thoughts race, I pray you may direct my attention to your face and upward to you. I ask that you may come and comfort me during this. Help me to remember that you, Jesus have already won my battles. I just need to sit with you much to find the serenity I need to surrender my struggles and rest in you. You comfort our souls every time. Help me to seek your word during this time.
In Jesus' mighty name I pray, amen.
Thank you Father God.

2 Timothy 1:7

PLANTING WITH GOD
DAY 80

Prayer for Deliverance

Dear Father God, as I sit with you, I pray for deliverance. I have been plagued by such suffering that hinders my growth.
I pray that I may be delivered from the hand of my enemies and the devils schemes so my focus is solely on you. During times of suffering and attacks help me Jesus to run straight to you.
Lead me to cast out all of what is not of you to the bottomless pit.
Lord, I pray you may lead me to your words in the bible that shall be my shield during these times. Oh dear Lord, take my life by your hand and hold it dearly so I that I do not stumble into
plots against me that will keep me away from you. Lord, regardless of
anything that happens, I pray that I carry you with me so that if someone even
attempts to harm me, I am covered by the great armor of my Lord and Savior Jesus Christ.
In Jesus' mighty name, I pray amen.
Thank you God. hallelujah!!

**Psalm 32:7; Psalm 73:23;
Psalm 18:3**

PLANTING WITH GOD
DAY 81

Prayer for Help

Dear Father God, my strength and comfort at all times. Oh God, hear me, hear my wailing cries for help dear father. This is too much for me to bare and my hope has been hard to reach. But you oh God, I know will help me in your perfect timing.

Lord, I pray you help me continue to reach for you and believe that at any moment you can change things.
I pray you may be here with me during this to guide me along as I search for glimpses of you rescuing me. Lord, help me to remember to come to you and to seek your word always. Lead my way God, as without you I would go astray. Be with me, oh help me Lord. I weep so much during my despair and pray for your quick rescue, I know you are there.
In Jesus' mighty name I pray, amen.

Thank you father God. I praise you, Lord Jesus.

Philippians 4:6-7

PLANTING WITH GOD
DAY 82

Prayer

Oh my dear Lord, how thankful I am to experience your love and keep you close with me as I travel this narrow path with you.
I am grateful to have this day to spend with you. Lord, I pray you continue to help me build my foundation and plant myself with you. The amount of love you have poured on me here is something I have sought but would have never believed could be found by planting myself with you. To hear, and be led each day by you is such a gift as I now see the growth in my relationship with you is what brings forth such change in my circumstances and life.

Not only that but interactions with loved ones as well so they too may experience the celebration of your great works in your children.

I see now peace and comfort can only be through you. Others seek and seek to find nothing but empty hearts, empty people, empty words and promises keeping us with a sinking hole further and further in our hearts. Little do they know all they have to do is simply sit and get to know you, and that hole is no longer a hole, but now "whole" and overfilled spilling out everywhere we go. All glory to you Lord for such miraculous gifts, we cannot even begin to explain.

Romans 5:1-2

PLANTING WITH GOD
DAY 83

Romans 8:28

Dear God, I am not quite sure where I'm headed in this walk or your plan for my life; however, since learning of you those questions and worldly wonders have started to fade. You have become wondrous in my life. Nothing compares to the love of Jesus.

The restoration of our entire being you can bring. In this world, all I ever wanted was to be is accepted by those around me, which has caused me to sometimes not even be my true self.
However, after coming to you, I see now you made me specifically for your purpose, great reasons and glory so that others too could find you. For us to live such a life with purpose, and now meaning through you, that sure is special. I will do my absolute best to share the gospel and all that I have learned through my time with you so they too can experience such joy, love and peace through being planted, watered, and fed by you.

What beauty you can bring through the process, and when they experience it they won't believe their eyes and that is something I truly don't want others to miss. My heart will share and my words will be plentiful and fullfilling when I speak of you.

PLANTING WITH GOD
DAY 84

2 Corinthians 5:17

Dear child, I see you. I know your heart, hopes, and desires. I speak to you in the silence of your heart when you rest it easily in my arms. I have you, and I will never lose my love for you. I appreciate so much those who seek to know me. I had already chose you, and awaited your return from the harsh world.

You have heard my call after all.
I do reveal myself to those I chose, who also choose my way and to seek me with much faith. I have so much to offer my children. Yet some choose to turn the other direction further and further away from me because it seems easy, only to stumble terribly. That other path is also not easy, and more difficult to follow with road blocks all over the earth by man.

As you travel this path with me there will be some difficulties but utilize my word, prayer, and sitting with and following me as I am your road map and shield.

I promise you will never get lost. In
fact you may learn much along the way for you to also share with others so they too can find thier way. Also while doing so I will gift you with much because you chose to renew your soul and travel through me.

PLANTING WITH GOD
DAY 85

The Lord says

Dear child, do you see what all I have been sprouting out of what was once dark and gloomy? Look at you bloom in such light once you came to grow with me. Trusting my process, sounds a little too simple to some, but it can completely allow for you to be a new version of yourself, the version I originally chose for you.

The consistent reliance upon me makes all the waiting and trials eventually seem beautiful when you finally get the opportunity to actually stop and notice me. Then you become ready to bloom and that process becomes delightful and worthwhile because my children can then see beauty out of despair, peace out of pain, and love out of brokenness. All of this takes time to repair as we grow and learn during every part of it. The long process becomes the beginning of wisdom and knowledge so we can assure we have learned much through it all allowing us to retain the gifts God has sent.

John 15:5

PLANTING WITH GOD
DAY 86

The Lord says

As we begin to grow together I promise meeting with me will become the priority. Never again shall it be considered a chore. When my children allow themselves time to bloom through my love, they will know it is I who can make each day new with much meaning for not only you but your family, brothers and sisters in Christ, and even unbelievers too. May they recognize the light I have placed in your eyes and the Holy Spirit shining upon you. So they too can also see me. With each interaction recall my purpose here for you and you won't suffer through the daily mishaps.

You begin to learn some doors are closed ahead for protection, some to awaken you, and some closed to teach so that you may help the next. There's purpose in each and every experience.

Psalm 57:2

PLANTING WITH GOD
DAY 87

Prayer for Life's Battles

Dear God, you are
true and real.

You are felt, seen and heard by those who call out to you. I pray for the others safe return.

With you God is the best place we can plant ourselves. Through the weight of our troubles only God can allow us the peace we need to continue to flourish for ourselves and others around us.

Life can be difficult, we must prepare and be ready, as we have set out to follow God's will for us, but the wicked run rampant here in this earth awaiting our foes, thinking we will turn away from God because of it. Once we have submitted ourselves to God and armor ourselves daily, the devil must flee. He has been overcome. What a triumph.

Hallelujah, we thank you Lord Jesus.

James 4:7

PLANTING WITH GOD
DAY 88

Gratitude to God

To my dear loving Lord and Savior, Jesus Christ. Thank you for your love for us. I pray you may help me remember you with all that I do. May I always recall your great works, and remain grateful that in any moment I can invite you into my life.

Nothing has been accomplished by me, only by you. Help me to remember all you can do if I just stop, sit and rest easy with you.
Lord, I am grateful you allow me your presence and your loving peace and grace to us freely.
Thank you for my daily food that allows me to continue to bloom for you and your plans for my life. I pray you may help me to focus more on you and your word than anything on this earth so I may prosper in this walk for you. As you have allowed me this gift of life for your Glory, help me to lead the way for others too.

Lord, truly, thank you. I love you.

Psalms 63

PLANTING WITH GOD
DAY 89

The Lord says

My dear child, here we have experienced time well spent. Now I hope you see what it is like to keep a daily relationship with me.
I see so many of my children suffering, but refuse to come to me.
My ways are sufficient. My timing is chosen specifically for your path. Every breath in you is an occasion that is always worth celebrating.
Celebrate, sing holy praises and shout for the Glory of God shall rest upon you.
In any season—sunshine, rain, storms, pain, loss, sickness all of these are bound to happen in life. Yet if you have me with you, those obstacles will be handled with such love, healing care and grace as you process it. Understand my appropriate timing for all things, and continue to surrender your life to me daily. I create each one of you intentionally with a specific purpose and plan that you may at this time not understand. I ask that my children seek it, because in finding it, you will find your joy, serenity and all the love and comfort you could ever need through me. Plus such great understanding of my truth, plan and precise timing for everything.

Child, I love you, please stay.

PLANTING WITH GOD
DAY 90

The Lord says

Child, there may days
you feel like you have failed.
But remember with me you shall not
wilt. Plant yourself firmly back with me always.

"You are planting a garden, and that takes time to bloom."
-God

Your faith can overcome any obstacle you may face. Just as you trust a safe and dear loved one, put that trust and more into me.
People will fail you, even those loved ones so cling to me rather than others.
If you choose me, you will always shine bright.
Regardless of what season you may be in
the sun shall shine bright again.
The seasons will change, but I am forever the same.

Do not lack belief when you pray, ask and believe it has been done.

Well fed souls and prayers also bloom in due season, but it takes much nourishing and belief.

Mark 5:34; Matthew 21:22

PLANTING WITH GOD

I pray this book has blessed you, and those whom you may share it with. It has truly blessed me in my walk with Jesus.

We have been through the trenches, and if you are here you too have most likely experienced much of the heartaches of tragedy, loss, grief, life and pain.
I completely understand this walk isn't easy, but let us continue to strive each day to cling to the hand of God. He has your purpose in his hands, we must strive to reach it.
God is the only one who will always hold us through everything and rise us up when we can't walk.

He has strengthened my roots, and bloomed me into someone I never knew, and now love.

If I can say one thing, it is:

"Keep Jesus and your bible near always."

Don't miss out on the most abundant gift of God and time with him.

Philippians 4:19

Psalm 17:6-7 (nKJv)

I have called upon you, for you will hear me, O God; Incline your ear to me, and hear my speech. Show your marvelous loving-kindness by your right hand, O You who save those who trust in you from those who rise up against them.

Jesus

PLANTING WITH GOD

I will triumph in the works of God's hands.

Psalm 92:4 (nkjv)

PLANTING WITH GOD

Those who are planted in the house of the Lord shall flourish in the courts of our God.

Psalm 92:13
(nkjv)

PLANTING WITH GOD

Yes, I will rejoice over them to do them good,
And I will assuredly plant them in this land, with all My heart and with all My soul.

Jeremiah 32:41
(nkJv)

·

thank you,
Jesus

PLANTING WITH GOD

PLANTING WITH GOD

Child,
I love
you.

-God

PLANTING WITH GOD

Made in the USA
Coppell, TX
21 February 2026

72218767R00066